STYRACOSAURUS

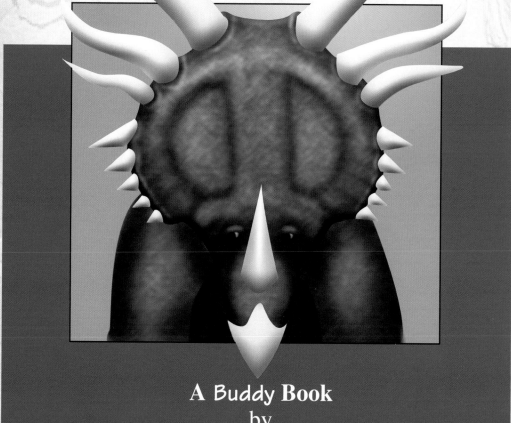

A Buddy Book
by
Christy Devillier

ABDO
Publishing Company

VISIT US AT

www.abdopub.com

Published by ABDO Publishing Company, 4940 Viking Drive, Edina, Minnesota
55435. Copyright © 2004 by Abdo Consulting Group, Inc. International copyrights
reserved in all countries. No part of this book may be reproduced in any form without
written permission from the publisher.

Printed in the United States.

Edited by: Michael P. Goecke
Contributing Editor: Matt Ray
Graphic Design: Denise Esner, Maria Hosley
Image Research: Deborah Coldiron
Illustrations: Deborah Coldiron, Denise Esner
Photographs: Corel, Digital Vision

Library of Congress Cataloging-in-Publication Data

Devillier, Christy, 1971-
    Styracosaurus/Christy Devillier.
       p. cm. -- (Dinosaurs)
    Includes index.
    Summary: Describes the physical characteristics, habitat, and behavior of a giant,
plant-eating dinosaur that is famous its spikes and horns.
    Contents: What were they?—How did they move?—Why were they special?
—Where did they live?—Who else lived there?—What did they eat?—
The family tree—Discovery—Where are they today?
    ISBN 1-59197-540-9
    1. Styracosaurus—Juvenile literature. [1. Styracosaurus. 2. Dinosaurs.] I. Title.

QE862.O65 D485 2004
567.915—dc22

                                               2003057815

TABLE OF CONTENTS

The Styracosaurus was a big, plant-eating dinosaur. It lived about 75 million years ago. The Styracosaurus is famous for its spiked frill and horn.

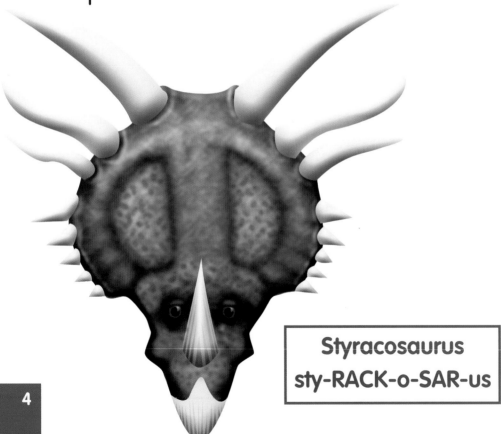

Styracosaurus
sty-RACK-o-SAR-us

The Styracosaurus may have been about 18 feet (five m) long. It probably stood about six feet (two m) tall. The Styracosaurus weighed about 6,000 pounds (2,700 kg). It was as heavy as a rhinoceros.

The Styracosaurus was as heavy as a rhinoceros.

The Styracosaurus walked on four short legs. It had five toes on each foot. The Styracosaurus could probably run fast. Scientists believe it ran as fast as 20 miles (32 km) per hour.

TAIL

FRILL

LEGS

BEAK

7

The Styracosaurus had a frill on the back of its head. This frill was hard and made of bone. On the Styracosaurus's frill were six long spikes. Scientists named the Styracosaurus after these spikes. Styracosaurus means "spiked lizard."

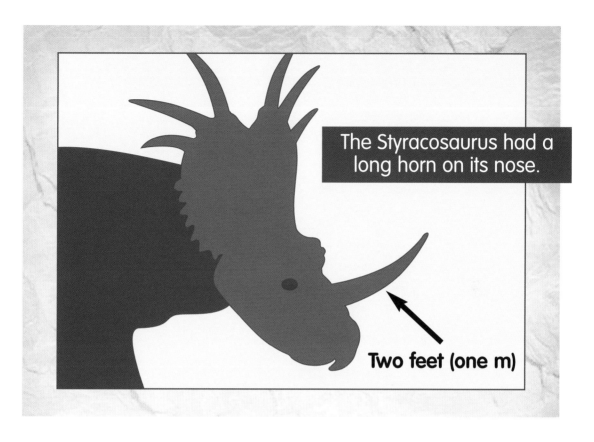

The Styracosaurus had a
long horn on its nose.

Two feet (one m)

The Styracosaurus had a hard
bump above each eye. It also had
a big horn on its nose. This horn
was about two feet (one m) long.
The Styracosaurus probably used
its spikes and horn to scare
away predators.

The Styracosaurus lived during the Cretaceous period. Back then, a shallow sea covered much of North America. It was called the Colorado Sea. The Styracosaurus lived west of the Colorado Sea. It lived on land that is now the United States and Canada.

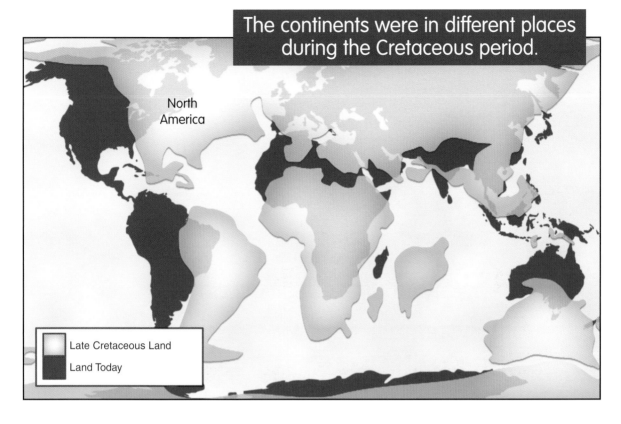

The continents were in different places during the Cretaceous period.

North America

Late Cretaceous Land

Land Today

The world was very different during the Cretaceous period. The weather was tropical. Forests covered the land. The forests were full of evergreens, palms, horsetails, and tree ferns. There were flowering plants, too.

WHO ELSE LIVED THERE?

The Styracosaurus lived among other animals. There were insects, such as ants, butterflies, and grasshoppers. Mammals lived in the forests. Birds and pterosaurs flew in the skies.

Pterosaurs were flying reptiles. One of the largest pterosaurs was the Quetzalcoatlus. Its outstretched wings were 43 feet (13 m) across.

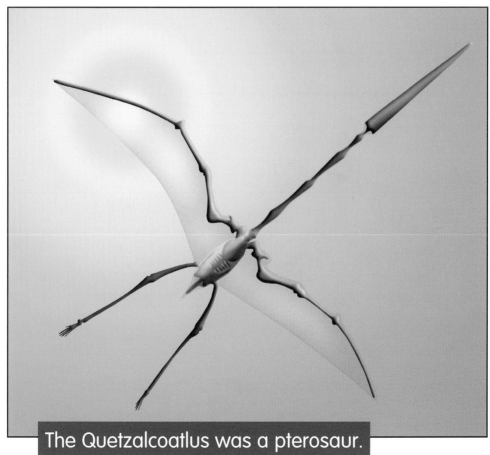

The Quetzalcoatlus was a pterosaur.

Many kinds of animals lived in the oceans. There were giant turtles, fish, and ammonites. Ammonites lived in shells. They are not around today.

The Styracosaurus lived among other dinosaurs, too. One was the Corythosaurus. The Corythosaurus was a duck-billed dinosaur. It ate plants with a hard beak. The Corythosaurus also had a special crest on its head.

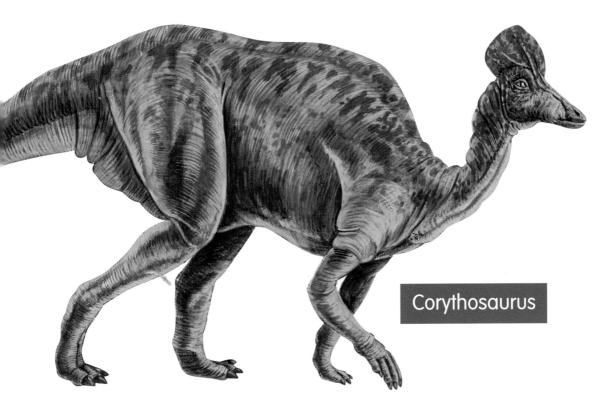

Corythosaurus

The Corythosaurus was bigger than the Styracosaurus. It was about 30 feet (nine m) long. The Corythosaurus may have weighed about 10,000 pounds (4,500 kg). That is as heavy as an elephant.

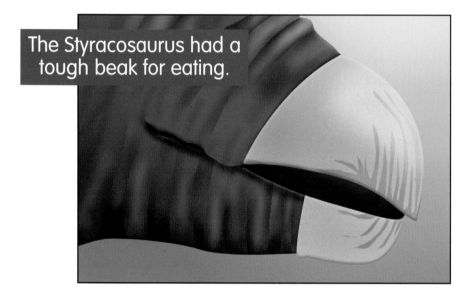

The Styracosaurus had a tough beak for eating.

The Styracosaurus ate plants. It probably ate palms and other plants. The Styracosaurus ate with a tough beak. It chewed food with special teeth in its cheeks.

The Styracosaurus ate plants.

The Styracosaurus lived among many meat-eating predators. One was the Dromaeosaurus. It was much smaller than the Styracosaurus. The Dromaeosaurus was about six feet (two m) long. It weighed about 33 pounds (15 kg).

Dromaeosaurus

The Dromaeosaurus may have
hunted in packs. Scientists believe
they were fast runners, too. Maybe
they hunted the Styracosaurus's young.

Scientists believe the Styracosaurus lived in groups called herds. Living in herds was safer than living alone. The Styracosaurus could warn each other when danger was near.

The Styracosaurus could use its spiked frill and horn to defend itself. Maybe it acted like today's rhinoceroses. They charge predators that come too close.

A rhinoceros uses its large horn to defend itself.

THE FAMILY TREE

The Styracosaurus was a ceratopsian dinosaur. It belonged to the Ceratopidae family. All the ceratopsian dinosaurs ate plants. Most of them had horns and frills.

Another ceratopsian was the Protoceratops. It lived about 70 million years ago. The Protoceratops had a hooked beak and no horns.

The Protoceratops was smaller than the Styracosaurus. It was about seven feet (two m) long. The Protoceratops weighed about 900 pounds (400 kg).

The Protoceratops was a ceratopsian dinosaur.

Three Ceratopsian
Dinosaurs

Protoceratops

Styracosaurus

Triceratops

Paleontologists study fossils. Fossils help paleontologists understand what dinosaurs were like. People have found Styracosaurus fossils in Montana and Alberta, Canada.

One time, people found many Styracosaurus fossils in one place. The bones belonged to about 100 Styracosaurus dinosaurs. Why were so many Styracosaurus dinosaurs in one place? Paleontologists think these dinosaurs must have lived together. They believe the fossils belonged to a Styracosaurus herd.

Paleontologists study dinosaur fossils such as this one to learn about dinosaurs.

L.M. Lambe was a paleontologist. He studied Styracosaurus fossils found near Alberta, Canada. He named the Styracosaurus in 1913.

American Museum of Natural History
Central Park West at 79th Street
New York, NY 10024-5192
http://www.amnh.org/

The Canadian Museum of Nature
Victoria Memorial Museum Building
240 McLeod Street (at Metcalfe Street)
Ottawa, Ontario, Canada
http://nature.ca/nature_e.cfm

STYRACOSAURUS

NAME MEANS	Spiked lizard
DIET	Plants
WEIGHT	6,000 pounds (2,700 kg)
LENGTH	18 feet (5 m)
TIME	Late Cretaceous period
ANOTHER CERATOPSIAN	Protoceratops
SPECIAL FEATURE	Spiked frill
FOSSILS FOUND	USA—Montana Canada—Alberta

The Styracosaurus lived
75 million years ago.

The first humans appeared
1.6 million years ago.

Triassic Period	Jurassic Period	Cretaceous Period	Tertiary Period
245 Million years ago	208 Million years ago	144 Million years ago	65 Million years ago
Mesozoic Era			Cenozoic Era

29

WEB SITES

To learn more about the Styracosaurus, visit ABDO Publishing Company on the World Wide Web. Web sites about the Styracosaurus are featured on our "Book Links" page. These links are routinely monitored and updated to provide the most current information available.

www.abdopub.com

Cretaceous period a period of time that happened 144–65 million years ago.

dinosaur a reptile that lived on land 248–65 million years ago.

fossil remains of very old animals and plants commonly found in the ground. A fossil can be a bone, a footprint, or any trace of life.

mammal most living things that belong to this special group have hair, give birth to live babies, and make milk to feed their babies.

paleontologist someone who studies very old life, such as dinosaurs, mostly by studying fossils.

predator an animal that hunts and eats other animals.

reptile scaly-skinned animals that cannot make heat inside their bodies.

tropical weather that is warm and wet.

 INDEX